DK SUPER Planet

Look at these LANDFORMS!

Explore the breathtaking variety of landforms that shape our planet—from deep sea trenches, to vast plateaus, to the highest mountains on Earth

Produced for DK by
Editorial Just Content Limited
Design Studio Noel

Author Nancy Raines Day

Senior Editor Amelia Jones
Senior Art Editor Gilda Pacitti
Managing Editor Katherine Neep
Managing Art Editor Sarah Corcoran
Production Editor Jaypal Chauhan
Production Controller Rebecca Parton
Publisher Sarah Forbes
Managing Director, Learning Hilary Fine

First American Edition, 2025
Published in the United States by DK Publishing,
a division of Penguin Random House LLC
1745 Broadway, 20th Floor, New York, NY 10019

Copyright © 2025 Dorling Kindersley Limited
25 26 27 28 29 10 9 8 7 6 5 4 3 2 1
001–345409–Mar/2025

All rights reserved.
Without limiting the rights under the copyright reserved
above, no part of this publication may be reproduced, stored
in or introduced into a retrieval system, or transmitted, in any
form, or by any means (electronic, mechanical, photocopying,
recording, or otherwise), without the prior written permission
of the copyright owner.
Published in Great Britain by Dorling Kindersley Limited

A catalog record for this book
is available from the Library of Congress.
HC ISBN: 978-0-5939-6258-9
PB ISBN: 978-0-5939-6257-2

DK books are available at special discounts when purchased
in bulk for sales promotions, premiums, fund-raising,
or educational use.
For details, contact: DK Publishing Special Markets,
1745 Broadway, 20th Floor, New York, NY 10019
SpecialSales@dk.com

Printed and bound in China

www.dk.com

Contents

Earth's Terrain	4
Plate Tectonics	6
Continents and Oceans	8
Volcanoes	10
Mountains	12
Ocean Trenches	14
Geysers and Hot Vents	16
Natural Hazards	18
Erosion and Deposition	20
Shoreline Features	22
Glaciers and Fjords	24
Valleys, Canyons, and Gorges	26
Plains, Prairies, and Plateaus	28
Hot Deserts	30
Cold Deserts	32
Everyday Science: Exploring Energy Sources	34
Everyday Science: Exploring Fossils	36
Let's Experiment! Make a Volcano	38
Let's Experiment! Make a Wave-Maker	40
Vocabulary Builder: Describing Volcanoes	42
Glossary	44
Index	46

Words in **bold** are explained in the glossary on page 44.

Earth's TERRAIN

At 29,035 ft (8.85 km) above sea level, Mount Everest is the highest point on Earth. That's almost as high as airplanes fly. Above 26,000 ft (7.92 km), there's very little oxygen to breathe. Climbers must bring their own.

A distinct natural feature on Earth's surface is called a **landform**. Some landforms, like mountains and canyons, can be high or wide. Others, like hills and valleys, may be small or narrow. Together, landforms determine Earth's **terrain**—what it looks like and what kind of life it can support. Let's explore some of Earth's amazing landforms.

Strokkur is a geyser in Iceland. A geyser is a hot spring where steam and water regularly erupt. Strokkur erupts every 5–10 minutes. It can shoot water up to 131 ft (40 m) high in the air.

The Grand Canyon, in Arizona, is made up of many different rock layers. Over time, the layers have built up. This means the oldest rock layer is on the bottom. Some of the rocks in this layer are 1.8 billion years old.

The flattest area on Earth is the Uyuni salt flat in Bolivia. Satellites use it to check and adjust their altimeters—these are devices that measure distances above sea level. People have also set car racing records on the salt flat.

The Sahara, in Northern Africa, is the biggest hot desert on Earth. Most of the desert is rocky. It contains plains, plateaus, mountains, and sand dunes. The sand dunes can rise as high as 600 ft (182.88 m)—that's as tall as a 60-story building.

Plate TECTONICS

Earth's mantle is made up of very hot liquid and semiliquid rock. Huge slabs of broken rock float on top of the mantle. These slabs are called tectonic plates. Over millions of years, the plates have moved, forming **mountains**, **volcanoes**, and ocean basins. This is known as **plate tectonics**.

The San Andreas Fault is in California. It can be seen on Earth's surface in areas like the Carrizo Plain, where it appears as a series of ridges.

The San Andreas Fault is a good example of a transform fault. This is where two tectonic plates slide past each other in opposite directions. The San Andreas Fault is one of the largest faults on Earth. It formed about 30 million years ago.

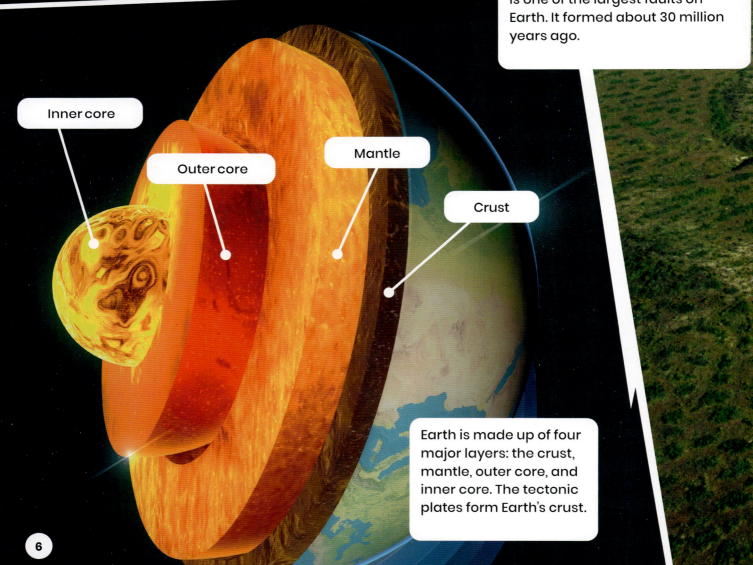

Earth is made up of four major layers: the crust, mantle, outer core, and inner core. The tectonic plates form Earth's crust.

The San Andreas Fault is between the Pacific and North American Plates. These plates are moving very slowly in different directions. But it adds up! Neenach Volcano was split by the fault. After 23 million years, the two halves of Neenach are 195 miles (313.82 km) apart.

The areas where the edges of tectonic plates meet are called **plate boundaries**. **Earthquakes** and volcanoes commonly occur here. There are three types of plate boundaries.

1 PULLING APART
When plates pull apart, very hot rock rises from the mantle to Earth's surface. The rock cools, forming new crust.

2 PUSHING TOGETHER
When plates collide, one plate can push up over the other. This can form mountains and volcanoes. One plate can push the other down, forming an ocean trench.

3 RUBBING ALONG
When plates slide past each other, landforms located on the boundary can be broken up and moved. **Rift valleys** or undersea **canyons** can form.

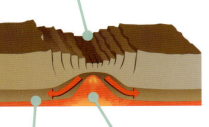

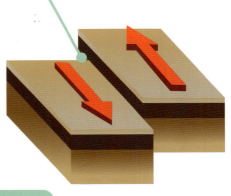

Continents and OCEANS

Earth has two primary landforms—**continents** and oceans. The seven continents are **North America**, **South America**, **Europe**, **Asia**, **Africa**, **Australia**, and **Antarctica**. Earth's five major oceans are the **Pacific Ocean**, **Atlantic Ocean**, **Arctic Ocean**, **Indian Ocean**, and **Southern Ocean**. But Earth didn't always look like this.

Find out!

Pick a continent and research its ancient past. What did the continent look like millions of years ago? How has it changed over time?

1 From about 300–200 million years ago, all Earth's land was joined together in a supercontinent. It was called Pangaea, which means "all lands." Pangaea was surrounded by an ocean called Panthalassa.

2 Over time, the tectonic plates moved and broke Pangaea up into smaller pieces of land. They moved away from each other. Separate oceans began to form.

3 These pieces of land eventually formed the continents and oceans as we know them today. This includes the land of the **North Pole** and the **South Pole**.

Fascinating fact

The Atlantic Ocean is growing. As the tectonic plates underneath it move apart, the ocean is getting wider. It gains about 1.6 inches (4 cm) a year.

4 Earth's plates are always moving. Scientists predict that all the continents will come together again 250 million years from now.

VOLCANOES

A volcano is an opening, or vent, in Earth's crust where molten rock, hot ash, and gases can erupt from. Volcanic eruptions can last for days, months, or even years. Volcanoes can destroy anything in their path. But they can also create mountains and islands, and make the land **fertile**.

Mauna Loa in Hawai'i is the world's largest active volcano. An active volcano is still erupting, but many years can pass between eruptions.

Find out!

How did the 1815 eruption of Mount Tambora in Indonesia cause a "year without summer"? How did it affect the weather and crops in Europe and the US?

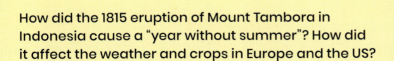

It blocked the sunlight with gas and ash. This made the weather cold, which ruined crops.

A volcano that currently shows no signs of activity is called dormant, which means "sleeping." Mount Kilimanjaro in Africa is a dormant volcano.

When a volcano erupts, **magma** comes up through cracks in the plate. On Earth's surface, magma rises as **ash** and runs down as **lava**. After cooling by time and weather, the lava hardens into **lava rock**. As a result, each time the volcano erupts, it grows in size.

Ash

Lava

Lava rock

Magma

Mount Vesuvius in Italy erupted in 79 CE. Ash and lava rocks spewed 21 miles (33 km) into the air. The eruption buried the city of Pompeii.

VOLCANO WARNING SYSTEMS

Humans can't stop volcanoes and natural hazards, but we can take steps to reduce their impact. Scientists use tools to monitor activity levels in volcanoes, so they can predict future eruptions.

11

MOUNTAINS

Volcanoes are one way that mountains can form. But they also form through plate tectonics. When the plates under different continents collide, they can buckle and fold. This pushes the land up, forming a **mountain range**. Over time, as the plates keep pressing against each other, the mountains get taller.

The Rocky Mountains in North America were formed more than 55 million years ago when pieces of the Earth's crust were pushed underneath each other.

Fascinating fact

Mountains exist under the sea, too. The Mid-Atlantic Ridge, the longest mountain range on Earth, is 90 percent underwater.

The Rocky Mountains are the largest mountain range in North America. They stretch from western Canada all the way to New Mexico. The climate in the Rocky Mountains goes from cold, snowy winters to mild summers. In the highest areas, there is snow on the mountain **peaks** year-round.

A gold rush in the early 1860s jump-started the first industry in the Rocky Mountains. Silver, copper, natural gas, and other minerals have been mined there too.

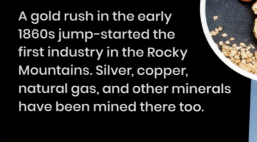

The other major industries in the Rocky Mountains are agriculture and forestry. In the summer, livestock like cattle graze in high-up pastures.

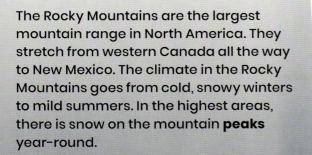

In the spring and summer, elk graze high in the Rocky Mountains. They come down to the meadows in fall and winter. Starting in spring, the males' antlers can grow 1 inch (2.5 cm) a day. They fall off each winter.

Black bears are the only bears left in the Rocky Mountains. They catch fish, but they mostly eat plants like fruits and nuts. To prepare for hibernation, they consume 20,000 calories a day.

Ocean TRENCHES

Ocean trenches are undersea **valleys** in the deep ocean floor. The lowest point on Earth is in the Mariana Trench in the Pacific Ocean, 6.86 miles (11 km) below sea level. That's as deep below sea level as some airplanes fly above ground.

Japan Trench

Tonga Trench

Mariana Trench

Ocean trenches are formed at tectonic plate boundaries, where one plate has pulled another one down. Ocean trenches are usually found near islands, volcanoes, and mountains.

The Ring of Fire is a string of volcanoes that follows the edges of the Pacific Ocean. You can also find the Mariana Trench, Tonga Trench, and Japan Trench here. These are some of the world's deepest ocean trenches. The Ring of Fire is also where about 90 percent of Earth's earthquake activity occurs!

Tectonic plate 1

Tectonic plate 2

14

Deep-sea trenches are home to many strange and fascinating creatures found only in the cold, dark, high-pressure environment of the deep ocean.

Zombie worms eat whale bones that fall to the sea floor.

Find out!

The deepest part of the Mariana Trench is called Challenger Deep. Can you find out who reached Challenger Deep first, and when?

Don Walsh and Jacques Piccard, 1960.

Anglerfish attract prey using their own light in the darkness.

Most octopuses have an ink sac, which releases ink into the water to help them avoid predators. However, the Dumbo octopus doesn't need one. This is because it has very few predators in the deep ocean.

Snailfish hold the record for the deepest fish. They have been found more than 5 miles (8 km) below sea level in the Izu-Ogasawara Trench in Japan.

Geysers and HOT VENTS

Geysers and **hot vents** are both types of hot spring. Water is heated naturally underground and then erupts through the surface. They are often found in areas with volcanic activity. Geysers are found on land and hot vents are found on the ocean floor.

GEYSERS

Geysers form when water underground is superheated by magma. The hot water starts to rise to the surface through different underground channels. This creates pressure. As the water gets closer to the surface, the pressure drops. The geyser erupts, shooting out hot water and steam.

Fascinating fact

The world's tallest active geyser is Steamboat Geyser in Yellowstone National Park. Its eruptions can shoot water more than 300 ft (91 m) into the air.

Old Faithful, a geyser in Yellowstone National Park, erupts around every 90 minutes—that's more often than any other big geyser.

HOT VENTS

Hot vents form when seawater seeps through cracks in the ocean floor. The cracks form in places where the plates are pulling apart. The magma under the plates superheats the water. The water and minerals in the magma shoot out of the cracks through a vent. This can form black smoker vents or white smoker vents.

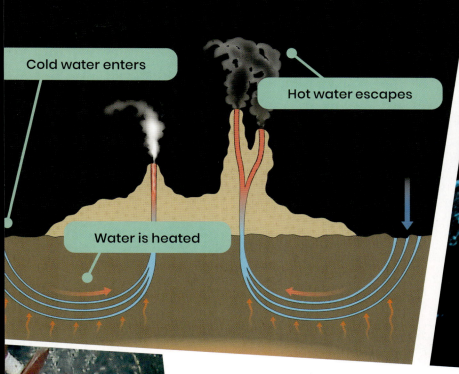

Cold water enters

Hot water escapes

Water is heated

Water temperatures in black smoker vents can reach 750°F (400°C). Because of the extreme pressure, the water stays in liquid form.

Scientists first discovered a hot vent in 1977. They are still learning about the unusual creatures to be found here. Since plants need light to survive, only animals can live around hot vents.

Giant tubeworms rely on bacteria to survive. The bacteria use chemicals from the vents to make sugar. Many other animals living near the vent rely on this sugar to survive, too.

Yeti crabs were discovered in 2005. They use the bristles on their pincers to gather and eat bacteria. Yeti crabs pile on top of each other. They survive by staying the perfect distance from the vents: not so far that it's too cold, and not so close that it's too hot.

Natural HAZARDS

When Earth's crust suddenly moves, it can cause an earthquake or a **tsunami**. Most earthquakes are so small that people don't even feel them. But powerful earthquakes can cause dramatic natural events, like landslides and flooding. Similarly, most tsunamis are small and don't cause much damage. However, bigger tsunamis can be very dangerous.

The Great Alaska Earthquake of 1964 is the second largest earthquake on record. It occurred where the Pacific Plate slides under the North American Plate. Cracks called ground fissures opened up. A section of the continental plate was lifted 30 ft (9.14 m). This raised parts of the coastline.

EARTHQUAKES

1 **Fault lines** are cracks in Earth's crust between tectonic plates.

2 Tectonic plates can move against or pull apart from each other. This movement is usually very slow.

3 If the ground moves suddenly, it can release a **seismic wave** through Earth. This causes an earthquake.

In 2004, an underwater earthquake occurred near the coast of the Indonesian island of Sumatra, shown in the picture above. This triggered a devastating tsunami. It reached coastal areas as far away as East Africa.

Scientists use different types of monitoring equipment to try to keep people safe. Earthquake monitoring and tsunami warning centers have been set up around the world. Engineers can also build structures to withstand earthquakes.

TSUNAMIS

1 Most tsunamis are caused by underwater tectonic activity, such as earthquakes and volcanic eruptions.

2 When large areas of the ocean floor rise or sink, it causes the water above to move up and down. This can create a series of giant waves, known as a tsunami.

3 Large waves can rise to more than 100 ft (30.48 m). They can flood up to one mile (1.6 km) inland.

Erosion and DEPOSITION

Earth is shaped through **erosion**. This is when wind, water, ice, and living things break off and move pieces of rock and soil. As the broken pieces are put down somewhere else, they build up. This is **deposition**.

Erosion and deposition can create new landforms. For example, as ocean waves crash into mountains, the water wears away the rock and the erosion can form cliffs. As the ocean moves pieces of rock, deposition can form beaches.

Erosion formed the Cotahuasi Canyon in Peru. As the Cotahuasi River flowed between two mountains, the water slowly carved out the canyon. **Glaciers** helped too. It is one of the world's deepest canyons—about two times as deep as the Grand Canyon.

Mushroom rocks in the **desert** are an example of wind erosion. As winds blow around sand, it hits the rock. The sand wears away the rock's base. This makes the rocks wide at the top and narrow at the bottom.

Plants and animals can also change Earth's surface. Plant roots can cause weathering when they grow into the ground and crack apart rocks they meet. Burrowing animals can contribute to erosion by moving soil and breaking up rock as they build their burrows.

Unlike most birds, burrowing owls nest in underground burrows instead of trees. They can be found in North and South America. Only some species dig their own burrows—most prefer to use burrows that have already been made by other animals.

Beavers build dams out of trees and branches that they cut using their strong teeth. Their dams slow down the flow of water and **sediment** in a **river** or stream. The sediment is deposited in the pond that the dam created. Over many years, this sediment can build up and eventually fill the pond.

Sand dunes are an example of deposition. The wind picks up and moves grains of sand, then drops them back on the ground. The sand builds up and forms dunes. The way the wind blows affects their shape.

21

Shoreline FEATURES

Erosion and deposition continuously shape Earth's terrain. Plate tectonics also shapes many of the landforms we see on Earth. These slow-moving, gradual processes form natural features on the land and near the shore. Some of these shoreline features include **bays**, **peninsulas**, **gulfs**, and **alluvial plains**.

Ha Long Bay is a famous natural harbor in northern Vietnam. It formed over hundreds of millions of years.

Rivers carry bits of rock carved from mountains. As the rivers flood over time, they deposit the rocks on flatter land. This forms alluvial plains. The alluvial plain surrounding the Nile, Egypt, is very fertile. It has provided food for Egyptians for the past 5,000 years.

Bays and peninsulas form as a result of coastal erosion. A peninsula is land mostly surrounded by water that sticks out from the mainland. Bays are water that is mostly surrounded by land.

Peninsula

Bay

1 As waves crash into the coast, the water breaks off pieces of soft rock.

2 As the soft rock erodes, a bay is formed.

3 If the rock is deposited along the coast, it can help build up and form a peninsula.

The Gulf of Mexico formed around 200 million years ago. The Florida peninsula is on the eastern shore.

Gulf of Mexico

Florida peninsula

Gulfs form as a result of plate tectonics. They form where Earth's plates have pulled apart. This creates a basin. Oceans then fill the basin, creating a gulf.

23

Glaciers and FJORDS

In very cold climates, the snow on mountain tops stays **frozen** year-round. Over time, the snow builds up in layers. This forms glaciers—huge masses of snow and ice. As glaciers move downhill, they gouge out chunks of rock, slowly transforming the **landscape**.

Humpback whales feed in Glacier Bay, Alaska, in the summer. Even though they are the size of a school bus, they can launch themselves right out of the water.

As a glacier creeps downhill, it carves out deep U-shaped valleys. These form glacial troughs on land. On the coast, they form **fjords**.

Glacier Bay National Park is in Alaska. Around 20,000 years ago, the park would have been covered in glaciers. You can find **glacial troughs**, valleys, and fjords here.

Find out!

Some glaciers are massive. Can you find where Earth's biggest glacier is? How many miles long is it? How many miles wide?

Lambert Glacier in Antarctica. 250 miles long, 60 miles wide.

Sea otters live in salt water, including fjords. They are aquatic animals, which means they do not live on land. Almost 90 percent of the world's sea otters live in Alaska.

When seawater floods the deep U-shaped valleys that glaciers form, this creates a fjord. Norway is famous for its many fjords—it has around 1,190. But there are also fjords in Alaska, Canada, Greenland, Chile, and New Zealand.

Valleys, Canyons, and GORGES

A valley is any low spot surrounded by higher ground. But the word is normally used for places where a river or glacier has eroded rock over time. Valleys come in many shapes and forms. This includes rift valleys, canyons, and **gorges**.

VALLEYS
A river flows downhill from a mountain. Over time, water floods the riverbank. The river water erodes the land. This leaves behind a valley.

RIFT VALLEYS
A rift valley is low land. It forms where two tectonic plates are pulling apart. The Rio Grande in Texas and the Rhine Valley in Germany are both rift valleys.

The Nubian Plate and the Somali Plate are pulling apart from each other. Over time, this has formed the East African Rift System, which includes rift valleys like this one in Kenya.

CANYONS

A canyon is a steep and narrow valley. It starts as a high, flat plateau. The soft rock layers that make up the plateau erode. The hard rock remains, forming the canyon.

The Colorado River eroded layers of sandstone, limestone, and harder rock. This process shaped the spectacular Grand Canyon. In some spots, the canyon is more than 1 mile (1.6 km) deep.

GORGES

A gorge is also steep and narrow. It may be bordered by uplifted mountains and often has a stream or river running through it.

The Columbia River Gorge was carved out by flooding caused by melting glaciers. It is located between Washington and Oregon.

27

Plains, Prairies, and PLATEAUS

Wide, flat, empty landscapes are found across all continents of the Earth. **Plains** and **prairies** are formed in similar ways. A different process creates dramatic, raised plateaus.

PLAINS

A plain is a wide, mostly flat grassland with few trees. The **horizon** stretches as far as the eye can see. Grass can survive the hot, dry summers and cold winters.

Plains are formed by erosion and deposition. Water and ice carry bits of rock and dirt from higher ground, such as a mountain. The bits of rock are deposited in layers, which creates a plain. Plains are found on every continent.

The Great Plains contain parts of ten US states and three Canadian provinces. They cover 1.2 million sq miles (3 million sq km). The land is often used by farmers for growing crops.

PRAIRIES

Prairies are formed in a similar way to plains. But prairies may have rolling hills and they are not as dry. Prairies support tall grass, shrubs, and wildflowers.

Prairie dogs are native to the grasslands of North America. They live in mazes of underground tunnels called towns. One town can cover 0.5 sq mile (1.3 sq km).

The Pampas of South America are large grasslands. They are similar to North American prairies. Small herds of guanacos graze in the Pampas. They are wild relatives of llamas.

PLATEAUS

Plateaus are flat, raised areas. They are formed of horizontal rocks that were pushed up by colliding tectonic plates. The Deccan Plateau forms India's entire southern peninsula.

The Colorado Plateau covers parts of four states in the southeastern US. It includes Zion National Park, shown in the picture above, the Grand Canyon, and seven other national parks.

Hot DESERTS

The Sahara is home to many animals, including monitor lizards. Their bodies have adapted to the desert heat. When the temperatures get too cold, they hibernate.

All deserts are dry. An **arid** desert is one that is very dry, while a **semiarid** desert has some rainfall. Temperatures in hot deserts can top 100°F (38°C) during the day and drop to freezing at night.

The Sahara, in North Africa, is an arid desert. It is one of the largest and driest deserts on Earth. Hot deserts like the Sahara are a tough place for plants and animals to survive. Water can be hard to find across the scorching landscape.

Find out!

In many places on Earth, human activities have turned non-desert land into desert. This is called **desertification**. Can you find out how drought has affected people who live on the southern edge of the Sahara?

Drought has made it hard to grow crops and raise animals.

30

The Kalahari Desert in southern Africa is semiarid. It supports acacia trees, which giraffes eat. Lions, elephants, and flamingos are some of the 320 species of mammals and birds that live there.

You can find roadrunners in the Chihuahuan Desert, which is the largest in North America. Roadrunners are birds. They can run as fast as 15 miles (24 km) an hour. They get all the water they need from what they eat, including cactus fruit and other birds.

The Sonoran Desert is the hottest in North America. It has more than 2,000 species of plants. It is home to the saguaro cactus, which can grow over 40 ft (12 m) tall.

The San have lived in the Kalahari Desert for over 20,000 years. In the dry season, they collect water by sticking hollow grass stems into damp sand. The stems act like straws. They store the water in empty ostrich eggs.

Cold DESERTS

All deserts have very little or no rainfall. But not all deserts are hot. Some deserts have low temperatures. These are called cold or temperate deserts. Cold deserts are located at higher latitudes than hot deserts, which are found in tropical climates.

The Gobi Desert in Asia is the sixth largest desert on Earth. Gobi means "waterless place" in Mongolian. Only 5 percent of the Gobi Desert is covered with sand. The rest of the land is mostly bare rock or dry grasslands.

Camels in the Gobi have thick coats and store water in their humps to survive.

Frost and sometimes snow top the dunes in the Gobi Desert.

Fascinating fact

Ancient traders carried goods between Europe and Asia on the Silk Road. To cross the Gobi Desert, they banded together in caravans of camels. Camels can drink up to 30 gallons (113.5 liters) of water at a time.

The Great Basin Desert in the western US has cold, snowy winters and dry, hot summers. The desert's peaks and valleys are high in elevation.

The Patagonian Desert is found at South America's southernmost tip. Strong, constant winds blow cold air across the desert. It rarely gets warmer than 53°F (12°C).

Pumas here are bigger than in North America due to more prey for them to hunt.

Sagebrush is the main vegetation in the high valleys of the Great Basin Desert.

Pronghorn antelopes graze here. They can run at speeds up to 70 miles (113 km) an hour.

The Atacama Desert in Chile is the driest place on Earth. High mountain ranges surround it, blocking rain from the Pacific and Atlantic Oceans. The temperature ranges from 40°F to 70°F (4°C to 21°C) during the day. It can drop to freezing on winter nights.

Saltgrass, cacti, and even wildflowers live in the Atacama Desert.

33

Everyday SCIENCE
Exploring Energy Sources

Rocks called ores can contain important metals such as copper, gold, and iron. The picture above shows iron ore being mined from a pit and loaded onto a truck. The iron will be extracted from the ore in a large, hot container called a blast furnace.

Every material we use in our daily lives comes from Earth. This includes fossil fuels, such as oil and natural gas, and metals. All of these materials are found in or around rocks. We can mine metals from rocks. And we can find fossil fuels near rocks. This is because of how they form.

HOW DO FOSSIL FUELS FORM?

1 Millions of years ago, ancient plants and animals lived and died. Their remains were left behind.

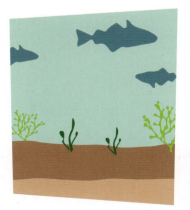

2 Layers of sediment formed over these remains. Pressure turned the sediment into rock. Over millions of years, the remains turned into fossil fuels.

3 When people find oil or natural gas, they use machines to drill through the rock to collect it.

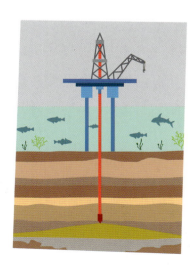

RENEWABLE ENERGY

Mining and burning fossil fuels produces harmful gases that cause pollution and contribute to climate change. By using renewable energy sources, we can reduce this and slow down climate change.

Hydroelectric dams like the Hoover Dam, which is on the border between Arizona and Nevada, are man-made landforms. They use water to generate electricity. When water runs through the dam, it spins a turbine connected to a generator that produces electricity.

When the sun shines onto a solar panel, energy is absorbed by special cells and converted into electricity.

Wind turbines use the power of the wind to create electricity. The wind makes the blades spin, and a generator converts this movement into electrical energy.

Everyday SCIENCE
Exploring Fossils

The study of plants and animals that lived millions of years ago is called paleontology. Scientists, known as paleontologists, study fossils to learn about life in the past.

Rocks aren't just a source of materials. They also provide clues to Earth's ancient past through fossils. Did you know there are lots of different kinds of fossils? Let's look at some of them.

CAST FOSSIL
This ammonite is a cast fossil. Ammonites are sea creatures. They went extinct about 66 million years ago. This fossil was found in layers of limestone rock.

MOLD FOSSIL
These ferns are mold fossils. They were found in layers of shale rock. A mold fossil shows the impression of a plant or animal.

PRESERVED REMAINS
This gnat is stuck in a piece of amber. Amber is fossilized tree resin (similar to sap). It often contains the preserved remains of insects.

TRACE FOSSIL
This 140-million-year-old dinosaur footprint is a trace fossil. A trace fossil shows ancient evidence of a plant or animal.

A team led by Egyptian scientists studied a fossil found in the Sahara, a vast desert that was an ocean 43 million years ago. In 2021, they identified the fossil as a new species of whale. It lived on land and sea.

The four-legged whale might have looked like this. Its webbed feet and powerful jaws allowed it to hunt prey on land and underwater. The discovery helps us see how this mammal went from a land-based plant eater to an ocean predator.

Hunting for fossils

You don't have to be a scientist to search for fossils. Go on a fossil hunt. Organize a trip to a natural history museum or science museum in your area. See how many different fossils you can spot.

Make your own fossil guide. Ask your teacher, friends, or family. Have they found any fossils? What kind? Where did they see them? Record their answers and draw the different fossils.

Let's EXPERIMENT!

MAKE A VOLCANO

When a volcano erupts, magma rises to Earth's surface and shoots out as lava. Did you know that you can make your own volcanic eruption using everyday items? Use the list of things you will need and follow the steps on the right.

You will need:
- A glass jar
- Vinegar
- Liquid dish soap
- Food coloring
- Baking soda
- A spoon

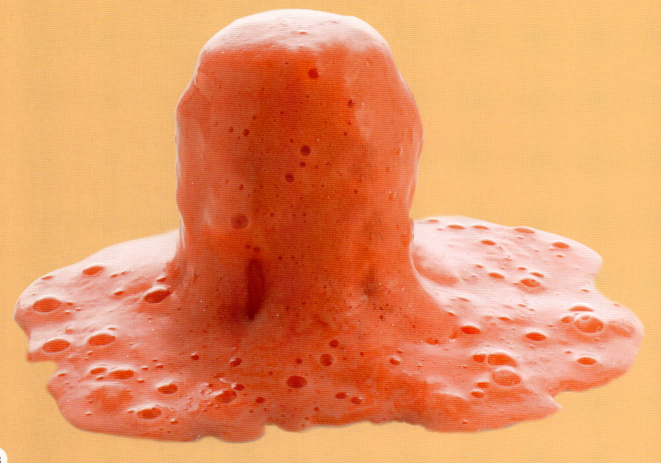

1 Half-fill a glass jar with vinegar. Add a few drops of liquid dish soap.

2 Add a few drops of food coloring to the mixture of vinegar and liquid dish soap and stir it.

3 Add a big spoonful of baking soda to the mixture and stir it.

4 Remove the spoon and stand back. Watch your volcano erupt!

KĪLAUEA VOLCANO

Kīlauea volcano is an active volcano in Hawai'i. It erupted in June 2024 after nearly 50 years. It first formed about 280,000 years ago, but it is still the youngest volcano in Hawai'i. The picture to the right shows lava erupting from the crater and flowing down the sides of the volcano.

Let's EXPERIMENT!

MAKE A WAVE-MAKER

Explore how ocean waves erode the coast by making your own wave-maker! Use the list of things you will need and follow the steps on the right.

You will need:
- A paint or baking tray
- Sand
- Small pebbles
- Water
- An empty bottle with a lid

1 Put an empty paint or baking tray on a flat surface.

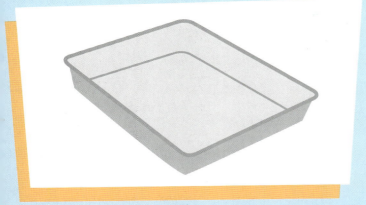

2 Add some sand to one end of the tray.

3 Put pebbles on the sand.

4 Pour the water in the empty end of the tray. Push the bottle down into the water and release it to make waves. What happens to the sand and pebbles?

COASTAL EROSION

Coastal erosion is the process where the power of the ocean crashing against the shore starts to wear the land away. It can cause dramatic changes to land next to the sea. It can erode land that is being used for roads, railways, or even housing.

Vocabulary BUILDER
Describing Volcanoes

One of the most destructive volcanic explosions ever recorded in North America was the eruption of Mount St. Helens in 1980. An earthquake triggered a landslide, which was followed by a blast of hot ash and rock that travelled about 15 miles (25 km) from the volcano.

Witnesses to the eruption included hikers, photographers, scientists, airplane passengers, and elementary school children on a camping trip. Read the eyewitness account below.

Mount St. Helens before the 1980 eruption.

> On May 18, 1980, I was 8 years old and lived about 20 miles from Mount St. Helens. The volcano had been bulging for weeks, but my parents said we weren't in the danger zone.
>
> I was playing outside when I noticed the birds stopped singing and it got really quiet. Then, at 8:30am, I heard three loud booms. I saw a gigantic, dark cloud coming quickly towards us. The sky turned black like night and there was a burning smell. It was really scary.
>
> We ran inside and shut all the doors and windows. Ash was falling from the sky, until the grass and our bikes were buried.
>
> We hid inside for a couple of days, watching the news coverage on the TV, until we were told it was safe to go outside. It took months to clean up all of the ash.

What did they describe?	air, ash, blast, cloud, crater, darkness, eruption, landslide, lava, lightning, magma, mountain, mud balls, mudflow, peak, plume, rock, slope, steam
How did they describe it?	active, angry, billowing, dormant, fiery, giant, gigantic, hot, massive, mighty, monstrous, mountainous, sheer, steep, thick, towering
What did it do?	blow, bury, collapse, darken, descend, destroy, eject, erupt, explode, flow, fork, heat, loom, rain, rise, smell, spew, spurt, vent

Clouds of ash billowed into the sky during the eruption.

The explosive eruption blew away the cone, or top, of the volcano. It lost over 1,300 ft (396 m) of its height and was left with a huge crater in the center.

Imagine you are witnessing a volcanic eruption. Write an eyewitness account like the one on page 42.

- What does it look like?
- What can you see?
- How do you feel?

Use the words in the vocabulary box above, and the photos on this page and on page 10 to help you.

Glossary

Alluvial plain A flat area of land formed by the deposition of sediment carried by a river.

Arid Very dry, with little to no rainfall.

Ash A mixture of rock fragments, minerals, and glass that results from a volcanic eruption.

Bay Water that is partially surrounded by a curve of land.

Canyon A very steep and narrow valley that may be bordered by mountains.

Continent One of the seven great landmasses on Earth.

Deposition A process caused by wind, water, and ice that deposits eroded material such as rock and sediment somewhere else.

Desert A dry landscape that can be hot or cold and does not have much vegetation.

Desertification A gradual process in which fertile land becomes desert, often due to human activity.

Earthquake The sudden shaking of Earth's surface, caused by seismic waves in Earth's crust.

Erosion A process caused by wind, water, and ice that wears away and transports material such as rock and sediment from one area to another.

Fault line A crack in Earth's crust where tectonic plates can move against or pull apart from each other.

Fertile Land that is good for growing crops.

Fjord A long strip of sea between steep hills or cliffs.

Frozen An adjective that describes a liquid that has become ice due to cold temperatures.

Geyser A hot spring where steam and water regularly erupt.

Glacial trough A deep U-shaped valley, formed by erosion from a glacier.

Glacier A huge piece of compressed snow and ice that slowly moves downhill, changing the landscape.

Gorge A valley that is steeper and narrower than a canyon.

Gulf Part of a sea or ocean that extends into land.

Horizon Where the land meets the sky.

Hot vent A hot spring on the ocean floor.

Landform A natural feature on Earth's surface that is part of the land.

Landscape The features of an area of land that can be seen.

Lava Very hot liquid or semiliquid rock found on Earth's surface as a result of a volcanic eruption.

Lava rock The rocks that are formed from lava.

Magma Very hot liquid or semiliquid rock found under Earth's surface.

Mountain A high, steep landform.

Mountain range A group of mountains that form a line and are connected.

North Pole The point the furthest north on Earth.

Peak The highest point of a mountain.

Peninsula A narrow piece of land that sticks out from the mainland and is surrounded by water.

Plain A wide expanse of mostly flat grassland with few trees.

Plateau A flat raised area.

Plate tectonics The theory that Earth's crust is made up of large, slow-moving plates.

Prairie A wide expanse of temperate grassland with few trees found in North America.

Rift valley A type of valley that is formed when two tectonic plates pull apart or move past each other, pulling the land apart and creating a rift.

River A waterway that typically starts at a source in the mountains and flows downhill to a mouth in the sea.

Sediment Small pieces of solid material like rocks, sand, and mud that are moved from one place to another.

Seismic wave A shock wave that travels through the ground, caused by an earthquake, explosion, or volcano.

Semiarid Dry, with some rainfall.

South Pole The point the furthest south on Earth.

Terrain An area of ground and how it is shaped.

Tsunami A giant wave caused by an undersea earthquake or volcanic eruption.

Valley An area of low-lying land, usually surrounded by higher ground, such as mountains.

Volcano A vent in Earth's crust where lava, hot ash, and gases erupt from, or have erupted from in the past.

Index

A
Africa 5, 8, 11, 19, 30
agriculture 13
alluvial plains 22–23
anglerfish 15
Antarctica 8
Arctic Ocean 8
ash 10–11, 42–43
Asia 8, 32
Atacama Desert 33
Atlantic Ocean 8–9, 33
Australia 8

B
bays 22–23, 24
bears 13
beavers 21

C
camels 32
canyons 4–5, 7, 20, 26–27, 29
Chihuahuan Desert 31
Colorado Plateau 29
Colorado River 27
Columbia River Gorge 27
continents 8–9, 12, 28
Cotahuasi Canyon 20
crust 6–7, 10, 12, 18

D
deposition 20–21, 22
deserts 20, 37
  cold 32–33
  hot 5, 30–31

E
earthquakes 7, 14, 18–19, 42
East African Rift System 26
elk 13
erosion 20–21, 22–23, 28, 41
Europe 8, 10, 32
experiments
  volcanoes 38–39
  waves 40–41

F
faults 6–7, 18
fjords 24–25
Florida 23
fossil fuels 34–35
fossils 36–37

G
geysers 16
Glacier Bay National Park 24
glaciers 24–25, 26–27
Gobi Desert 32
gorges 26–27
Grand Canyon 5, 20, 27, 29
Great Alaska Earthquake 18

Great Basin Desert 33
Great Plains 28
gulfs 22–23

H
Ha Long Bay 22
hazards, natural 11, 18–19
Hoover Dam 35
hot vents 16–17
humpback whales 24

I
Indian Ocean 8
inner core 6

J
Japan Trench 14

K
Kalahari Desert 31

L
landforms 4, 7, 8, 20, 22, 35
lava/lava rock 11, 38–39, 43

M
magma 11, 16–17, 38, 43
mantle 6–7
Mariana Trench 14–15
Mauna Loa Volcano 10
monitor lizards 30

mountains 4–7, 10, 12–13, 14, 20, 23, 27, 43
Mount Everest 4
Mount St. Helens 42
Mount Vesuvius 11

N
Neenach Volcano 7
Nile River 23
North America 7, 8, 12–13, 18, 29, 31, 33, 42
North Pole 9

O
oceans 8–9, 23
   trenches 7, 14–15
octopuses 15
Old Faithful Geyser 16
outer core 6
owls, burrowing 21

P
Pacific Ocean 8, 14
Pangaea 9
Patagonian Desert 33
peninsulas 22–23
plains 5, 6, 22–23, 28–29
plateaus 5, 28–29
plate boundaries 7, 14
plate tectonics 6–7, 12, 22–23

prairie dogs 29
prairies 28–29
pumas 33

R
renewable energy 35
Rhine Valley 26
rift valleys 7, 26
Ring of Fire 14
Rio Grande 26
roadrunners 31
rocks 5, 6–7, 10–11, 20–21, 23, 24, 26–29, 32, 34, 36, 42–43
Rocky Mountains 12–13

S
Sahara 5, 30, 37
San Andreas Fault 6–7
sand dunes 5, 21
San (people) 31
sea otters 25
shoreline features 22
snailfish 15
solar panels 35
Sonoran Desert 31
South America 8, 21, 29, 33
Southern Ocean 8
South Pole 9
Steamboat Geyser 16
Strokkur Geyser 4

T
tectonics see plate tectonics
terrain 4, 22
Tonga Trench 14
trenches, ocean 7, 14–15
troughs, glacial 24
tsunamis 18–19
tubeworms 17

U
Uyuni Salt Flat 5

V
valleys 4, 7, 14, 25–27, 33
volcanoes 6–7, 10–11, 12, 14
   describing 42–43
   experiment 38–39

W
wave experiments 40–41
whales 15, 24, 37
wind turbines 35

Y
yeti crabs 17

Z
zombie worms 15

Acknowledgments

The publisher would like to thank the following for their kind permission to reproduce their photographs:

(Key: a-above; b-below/bottom; c-center; f-far; l-left; r-right; t-top)

123RF.com: Sayompu Chamnankit 36br, Nataliya Hora 33b, Prapan Ngawkeaw 34, 36b, Dmytro Nikitin 34tr, smileus 35br, Sara Winter / sarawinter 5r, wrangel 29tr; **Alamy Stock Photo**: Accent Alaska 13tr, AP Photo / Nariman El-Mofty 37tr, Tom Bean 6-7, Carl Corbidge 30cra, Everett Collection Inc / © Buena Vista Pictures 15clb, funkyfood London - Paul Williams 5bl, Image Professionals GmbH / LOOK-foto 32, Mark Pearson 19tl, Adisha Pramod 15tl, 15bl, 17br, Science History Images 18cra, Science History Images / Photo Researchers 17tr, 17bl, Serenity 12l, Mike P Shepherd 22-23tc, Riley Shiery 21tr, Marko Steffensen 15cl, Rosanne Tackaberry 21br, Universal Images Group North America LLC / Planet Observer 22-23b, Alisa L. Gallant / USGS 10cl, USGS 42-43c, Jim West 28bl, World History Archive 43c; **Dorling Kindersley**: Colin Keates / Natural History Museum, London 36crb; **Dreamstime.com**: Andreistanescu 16, Andrey Bayda 4cb, Bennymarty 24b, Volodymyr Byrdyak 10-11, Chrisp543 19tr, Sorin Colac / Sorincolac 12-13b, Delstudio 35l, Pierre Jean Durieu 32cb, Frenta 11bl, Vera Golovina 20clb, Gary Gray 13tr (Mountains), Ivan Kmit 25b, MNStudio 27t, Jody Overstreet 25cr, Plotnikov 22bl, Ondřej Prosick 33tr, Martin Schneiter 20-21, Twildlife 33tl, Vampy1 6bl, Lawrence Weslowski Jr / Walleyelj 24cra, Björn Wylezich 36clb, Zaramira 31crb, Andreas Zeitler 30; **Getty Images**: Michele Falzone 5tl, John Finney Photography 29t, Nico De Pasquale Photography 29b, Thomas Roche 31b, Stone / Paul A. Souders 43cr, Jim Sugar 39br, The Image Bank / Richard T. Nowitz 36cra; **Getty Images / iStock**: 4nadia 27b, Matt Dirksen 12-13tc, EcoPic 31t, Sean Pavone 35tr, ratpack223 15r, sorincolac 25t, twildlife 31cla; **Shutterstock.com**: Steven J Taylor 41br

Cover images: *Front*: **Dreamstime.com**: Pablo Caridad br, Edwin Verin bl; **Getty Images / iStock**: DigitalVision Vectors / Sandipkumar Patel t; *Back*: **Alamy Stock Photo**: Tom Bean bl; **Dreamstime.com**: Plotnikov tl, Vampy1 cl